Catch

Written by D.C. Swanson
Illustrated by Clint Hansen

For Allie, Mom, and Dad - D.C.S.
"For you, I'll wait Willa Rose!" - C.H.

On summer evenings at the park
you'd find, before the day grew dark,
in some green field or grassy patch
a son and father playing catch.

The son would bring his ball and bat
and dusty little leaguer hat
and sit until he'd give a cheer
when he would see his dad appear.

The dad would keep his weathered mitt
inside his briefcase, where it fit
beside some papers that he'd shirk
to play some baseball after work.

They'd warm up first and then step back
to hear and feel the leather smack
as back and forth the fastballs flew
in humming arcs between the two.

And when they felt their fingers sting,
the dad would get the bat and swing.
He'd roll the sleeves up on his shirt
and hit some grounders in the dirt.

Then just before the sky got dark,
the dad would heave his highest arc
to watch his son go take a stab
at one last diving circus grab.

And once the final catch was done,
the dad would walk up to his son
who'd raise his glove above his cap
and give his father's mitt a tap.

But summer always turns to fall
and little leaguers soon grow tall
with far less time than they once had
for playing baseball with their dad.

At first, the son was all alone
among his friends without a phone.
He begged his parents to relent,
then screens were where his time was spent.

His dad got home one afternoon
and said the park is closing soon
but not just yet, and he would love
to hurry there and bring his glove.

The son said, "Dad, if it's ok,
I'd rather not play catch today.
Tomorrow then? This app is great!"
His father said, "For you, I'll wait."

Tomorrow, though, was back to school, and in this house, it was the rule that homework first must all get done before reserving time for fun.

The dad got home from work and asked the son to catch, but he'd been tasked with big assignments on his plate. His father said, "For you, I'll wait."

But once the schoolwork all got done,
the social scene ensnared the son
as webs of friendships spun and grew
and teenaged flirting started, too.

The dad brought out his glove and bat.
The son said, "Dad, the thing is that
tonight's the night I've got a date."
His father said, "For you, I'll wait."

Since high school living isn't cheap,
the son felt he should earn his keep
by working weekend shifts at stores
restocking shelves and sweeping floors.

With glove in hand, Dad tried to speak
but it had been a busy week.
The son said, "Dad, I'm working late."
His father said, "For you, I'll wait."

And soon, as sure as grass turns green,
the son grew up and turned eighteen
and made big plans that coalesced
to spread his wings and leave the nest.

The son said, "Dad, I wish there'd been
more time to throw like we did then,
but now I'm moving out of state."
His father said, "For you, I'll wait."

The son went off and built a life.
He served his country, found a wife,
and then, amazed how time had flown,
he had a daughter of his own.

Through spring and summer into fall,
the seasons seemed to spin, not crawl.
The son's and father's hair both grayed
and years passed by since they'd last played.

And then, one windy winter day,
his mother called the son to say,
"Your father's gotten very sick.
He's home in bed. And please come quick."

The son rushed home before the dark
to his old house beside the park.
He saw his mom and hugged her tight,
afraid of what they'd face that night.

He went upstairs where his dad was,
but paused outside the room because
his dad's old briefcase, worn and scratched,
was lying near the door, unlatched.

He picked it up to help make sure
that no one kicked it on the floor,
but it swung open just a bit
and from it fell his father's mitt.

The son then felt like time had stopped as he discovered what he'd dropped. He took the mitt and went inside and looked upon his dad and cried.

The son sat down and said through tears,
"We haven't had a catch in years.
I'm sorry, Dad, for it was wrong
for me to make you wait so long."

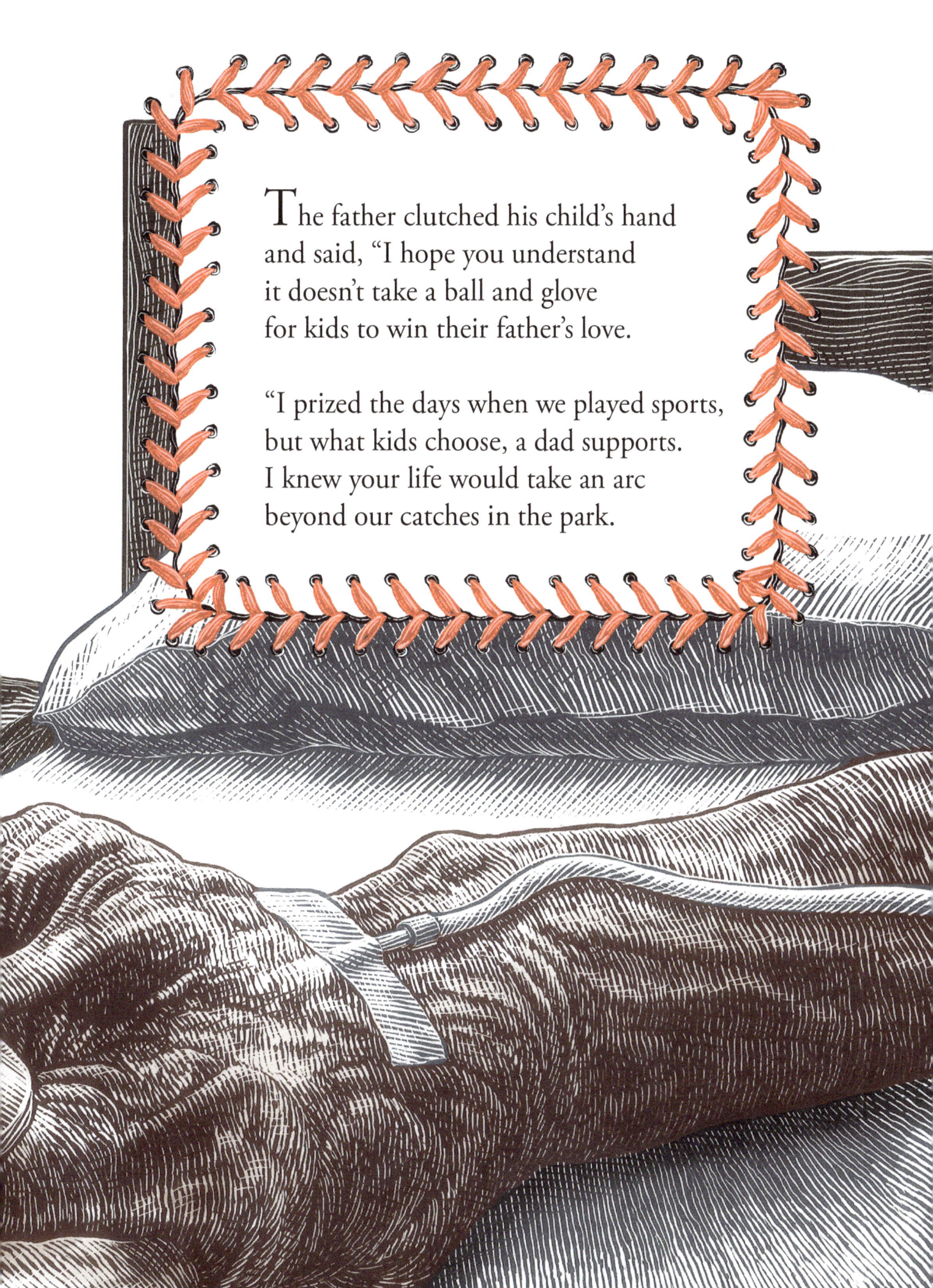

The father clutched his child's hand and said, "I hope you understand it doesn't take a ball and glove for kids to win their father's love.

"I prized the days when we played sports, but what kids choose, a dad supports. I knew your life would take an arc beyond our catches in the park.

"I'm proud of who you grew to be
and glad for all I got to see.
To watch you grow
and so much more—
son, that is what I waited for."

The son knelt down and bowed his head
and thanked his dad for what he'd said.
Then, wiping tears upon his sleeve,
he asked, "One thing, before we leave…"

He placed the mitt on his dad's hand,
then went to his old bedroom, and
got out his glove and dusty cap
and gave his father's mitt a tap.

When winter fades and spring returns,
each little leaguer soon relearns
what baseballs sound like when they smack
in gloves, and how to throw them back.

And one spring day, the son embarked
to take his daughter to the park
and give to her her granddad's mitt,
though it was far too big to fit.

He said, "Someday, if you so choose,
I think it might be fun to use
this glove to have a baseball catch
in some green field or grassy patch."

His daughter laughed when he was done and said, "Someday that might be fun, but I'm too small- I'm not yet eight!" Her father smiled. "For you, I'll wait."

© 2026 by D.C. Swanson
Illustrations © 2026 by Clint Hansen
All rights reserved. No part of this book may be reproduced, stored in a retrieval system or transmitted in any form or by any means without the prior written permission of the publishers, except by a reviewer who may quote brief passages in a review to be printed in a newspaper, magazine or journal.

The final approval for this literary material is granted by the author.

First printing

This is a work of fiction. Names, characters, businesses, places, events and incidents are either the products of the author's imagination or used in a fictitious manner. Any resemblance to actual persons, living or dead, or actual events is purely coincidental.

ISBN: 978-1-68513-736-6
Library of Congress Control Number:
PUBLISHED BY BLACK ROSE WRITING
www.blackrosewriting.com

www.ingramcontent.com/pod-product-compliance
Lightning Source LLC
LaVergne TN
LVHW072114060526
838200LV00061B/4887